Old MacDonald's Farm
Farm
Coloring Book

Cathy Beylon

DOVER PUBLICATIONS, INC.
Mineola, New York

NOTE

"Old MacDonald had a farm"—those words begin a popular children's song. In this coloring book, you will find pictures of Farmer MacDonald, Mrs. MacDonald, and Jacob and Emma, their children. Jacob and Emma usually wear work clothes on the farm, but they have just come back from a state fair and are dressed up. You will also see pictures of the farm animals that the MacDonalds live with. You will learn what many of the animals "say." Which one goes "Quack," and which goes "Neigh"? Read on to find out!

Have fun coloring in the pictures with crayons and colored pencils. When you are done, you will have learned quite a bit about Old MacDonald's farm.

Copyright

Copyright © 2003 by Cathy Beylon
All rights reserved.

Bibliographical Note

Old MacDonald's Farm Coloring Book is a new work, first published by Dover Publications, Inc., in 2003.

DOVER *Pictorial Archive* SERIES

This book belongs to the Dover Pictorial Archive Series. You may use the designs and illustrations for graphics and crafts applications, free and without special permission, provided that you include no more than four in the same publication or project. (For permission for additional use, please write to Permissions Department, Dover Publications, Inc., 31 East 2nd Street, Mineola, N.Y. 11501.)

However, republication or reproduction of any illustration by any other graphic service, whether it be in a book or in any other design resource, is strictly prohibited.

International Standard Book Number: 0-486-43034-0

Manufactured in the United States of America
Dover Publications, Inc., 31 East 2nd Street, Mineola, N.Y. 11501

Here is Old MacDonald on his farm. He is standing in
front of his barn, where he keeps hay.

Mrs. MacDonald has some flour and apples
to bake a pie.

Jacob and Emma wear their best outfits. They have just
come back from a state fair.

The family dog is running after some of Old
MacDonald's sheep. He cries, "Bow-wow!"

Snowball and her kittens live in the barn. They say,
"Meow, Meow."

Many birds make their home on Old MacDonald's farm.
The birds sing, "Tweet, Tweet."

6

The rooster gets up early. It cries, "Cock-a-doodle-do!"
and wakes up everyone.

The donkey on the farm makes a sound like "Hee-haw."

Oh, no! Some rabbits are eating the farmer's vegetables!
They'd better run.

The donkey has a job to do. It is pulling
a cart filled with hay.

These mice have found some corn in the barn.
Now they're having a tasty meal.

There is a pond on Old MacDonald's farm.
Here are some swans and a frog.

12

Ducks and their ducklings live on the farm. The ducks go, "Quack, Quack."

It's a hot day on Old MacDonald's farm.

These geese are going in and out of the pond to cool
off. The geese go, "Honk, Honk."

The hens and chicks pick grain from the
floor of the henhouse.

The hens say, "Cluck, Cluck." The chicks
go, "Cheep, Cheep."

There is plenty of room on the farm for horses.

These horses are munching on the grass.
They are eating apples, too.

Pigs eat their food in a special container.

What sound does a pig make? "Oink, Oink!"

The cows are eating grass and flowers out in the field.

The cows say, "Moo, Moo."

One of the farmer's dogs is trying to round up the lambs.

The sheep and their babies go, "Baa, Baa."

The goats are eating hay. They eat
many other things, too.

The goats say, "Naa, Naa."

Turkeys live on the farm. Look at their big feathers!

Turkeys make a silly sound—"Gobble, Gobble."

The MacDonalds hope that you enjoyed your visit to their farm. Good-bye!